2023-LOW ARB

Delicious and Simple Recipes for a

Healthier Home

Published By Nicholas Thompson

@ Jim Rowe

2023-Low Carb: Delicious and Simple Recipes for a Healthier Home

All Right RESERVED

ISBN 978-87-975002-4-8

TABLE OF CONTENTS

pan-Fried Spiced Crab Cakes With Remo Lade Sauce Recipe 1

Pan-Fried Coconut Curry Shrimp With Basmati Rice Recipe 4

Grilled Chicken Salad 7

Turkey Lettuce Wraps 9

Collard Wrap Burritos 11

Cheese Steak Stuffed Bell Peppers 14

Crumbed Asparagus 17

Air Fryer Vegetarian Pumpkin Schnitzel 19

Greek Style Air Fryer Shrimp Skewers 22

Crispy Buffalo Tofu Bites 24

Cheesy Chicken Bake With Zucchini 25

Bacon Chicken Alfredo 28

Zucchini Noodle Bowl With Turkey Meatballs 30

Grilled Shrimp And Avocado Salad 31

Slow Cooker Chicken Tikka Masala 34

Portobello Mushroom Burgers With Avocado 36

Grilled Eggplant Steaks With Chimichurri 39

Zucchini Noodles In Vegan Alfredo Sauce 40

Artichoke Hearts Stuffed With Goat Cheese 43

Eggs Stuffed With Guacamole 45

Green Olives Stuffed With Cream Cheese 48

Spicy Cajun Seafood Jambalaya Recipe 49

Moroccan Seafood Paella With Saffron Rice Recipe 53

Baked Salmon With Roasted Vegetables 56

Vegetable Stir-Fry With Tofu 58

Chicken Enchilada 60

Zucchini Chips 63

Cinnamon Nut Scrolls 65

Gluten-Free Salt And Pepper Tofu 67

Ranch Zucchini Fritters 70

Lemon Herb Air Fryer Tilapia 72

Mediterranean Eggplant Dip 73

Thyme Chicken Thighs 76

- Garlic & Ginger Chicken With Peanut Sauce 78
- Pork Chops With Cranberry Sauce 81
- Turkey Burgers With Avocado 82
- Greek Yogurt Chicken Salad 84
- Baked Halibut With Spinach And Tomatoes 86
- Coconut Curry Cauliflower Soup 87
- Green Beans With Toasted Almonds And Lemon 90
- Mashed Cauliflower With Garlic And Herbs 92
- Roast Chicken With Avocado Salsa 94
- Ham And Rocket Leaves 97
- Chicken And Vegetable Skewers 100
- Creamy Lemon Herb Salmon Pasta Recipe 103
- Spiced Seafood Fried Rice Recipe 106
- Quinoa Salad With Avocado And Black Beans 109
- Egg Salad Lettuce Wraps 111
- Lentil Soup 113
- Sweet Potato Fries 115
- Air Fryer Butternut Squash 117

- Ginger Soy Air Fryer Beef Stir Fry 118
- Spicy Air Fryer Cauliflower Bites 121
- Garlic Herb Air Fryer Pork Chops 123
- Pork Burgers With Caramelized Onion Rings 125
- Creamy Pork Chops 127
- Russian Beef Gratin 129
- Pumpkin Pie 131
- Cheesecake 133
- Chocolate Pudding 135
- Baked Avocado Fries With Sriracha Mayo 137

Pan-Fried Spiced Crab Cakes With Remo Lade Sauce Recipe

Ingredients:

- 2 tablespoons chopped fresh parsley
- 1 tablespoon Dijon mustard
- 1 teaspoon Old Bay seasoning
- 1/2 teaspoon paprika
- 1/4 teaspoon cayenne pepper (adjust to taste)
- Salt and black pepper to taste
- Vegetable oil for frying
- 1 pound lump crab meat
- 1/2 cup breadcrumbs
- 1/4 cup mayonnaise

- 1/4 cup finely chopped bell pepper

- 1/4 cup finely chopped red onion

- Lemon wedges for serving

Directions:

1. In a large bowl, gently combine the lump crab meat, breadcrumbs, mayonnaise, bell pepper, red onion, parsley, Dijon mustard, Old Bay seasoning, paprika, cayenne pepper, salt, and black pepper.
2. Be careful not to break up the crab meat too much.
3. Shape the mixture into crab cakes, about 3 inches in diameter.
4. Heat vegetable oil in a large skillet or frying pan over medium heat.
5. Working in batches, place the crab cakes in the skillet and cook for 3-4 minutes on each side until they are golden brown and crispy.

6. A slotted spatula transfers the cooked crab cakes to a paper towel-lined plate to drain excess oil.
7. Serve the spiced crab cakes hot, with sauce and lemon wedges.

Pan-Fried Coconut Curry Shrimp With Basmati Rice Recipe

Ingredients:

- 2 tablespoons curry powder
- 1 can (13.5 oz) coconut milk
- 1 cup chicken or vegetable broth
- 1 tablespoon fish sauce (optional) and 1 tablespoon brown sugar
- Salt and black pepper to taste
- 1 pound large shrimp, peeled and deveined
- 2 tablespoons vegetable oil
- 1 onion, finely chopped, and 2 cloves garlic, minced

- 1 tablespoon grated fresh ginger and 1 tablespoon ground turmeric
- Fresh cilantro for garnish and cooked basmati rice for serving

Directions:

1. Heat the vegetable oil in a large skillet over medium-high heat.
2. Add the chopped onion, minced garlic, and grated ginger to the skillet and sauté for 2-3 minutes until fragrant.
3. Add the curry powder and ground turmeric to the skillet and cook for another minute, stirring constantly.
4. Pour in the coconut milk and chicken or vegetable broth. Stir in the fish sauce (if using) and brown sugar—season with salt and black pepper to taste.

5. Bring the sauce to a simmer and cook for about 5 minutes to allow the flavors to meld together.
6. Add the shrimp to the skillet and cook for 4-5 minutes until they turn pink and opaque.
7. Remove from heat and garnish with fresh cilantro.
8. Serve the pan-fried coconut curry shrimp over cooked basmati rice.

Grilled Chicken Salad

Ingredients:

- Cherry tomatoes
- Cucumber slices
- Red onion slices
- Olive oil
- Lemon juice
- 4 oz grilled chicken breast
- Mixed salad greens
- Salt and pepper to taste

Directions:

1. Spice up the chicken breast with salt and pepper, then grill until cooked through.

2. In a bowl, mix the salad greens, cherry tomatoes, cucumber slices, and red onion slices.
3. Slice the grilled chicken breast and add it to the salad.
4. Sprinkle olive oil and lemon juice over the salad. Season with salt and pepper.
5. Toss everything together and serve.

Turkey Lettuce Wraps

Ingredients:

- Cabbage, shredded
- Green onions, chopped
- Soy sauce (low-sodium)
- Garlic powder
- Ginger powder
- 4 oz ground turkey
- Iceberg lettuce leaves
- Carrot, grated
- Sesame oil

Directions:

1. Heat a non-stick skillet over medium heat and cook the ground turkey until browned.
2. In a separate bowl, combine the grated carrot, shredded cabbage, and chopped green onions.
3. Add the cooked ground turkey to the bowl and mix well.
4. Season with soy sauce, garlic powder, ginger powder, and a few drops of sesame oil.
5. Spoon the turkey mixture onto individual lettuce leaves and wrap them up.
6. Serve immediately.

Collard Wrap Burritos

Ingredients:

- 2 cups of Monterey Jack cheese
- 15 oz. of black beans (cooked)
- ½ cup of cilantro
- 1 avocado (chopped)
- 1 teaspoon of chili powder
- 1 teaspoon of garlic powder
- Kosher salt
- Black pepper powder
- 1 cup of cherry tomatoes (chopped)
- 1 cup of frozen corn
- 4 big leaves of collard

- 1 tablespoon of olive oil

- 1 teaspoon of cumin (grounded)

- 1 lemon (juiced)

- 1 lb. of beef (grounded)

Directions:

1. Heat oil in a pan over medium heat.
2. Add the ground beef to the pan and cook until browned, breaking it up with a spoon. Cook until the pink color disappears. Strain out any excess fat.
3. Return the pan to the heat and stir in the garlic powder, salt, chili powder, cumin powder, and black pepper to season the beef.
4. Spread a layer of shredded cheese over the beef mixture in the pan. Cover the pan with a lid and cook for 2-3 minutes, or until the cheese has melted.

5. Meanwhile, prepare the collard leaves by placing them on a clean chopping board. Remove the thick midrib from each leaf.
6. Take 2 collard leaf and place 1/4th of the beef mixture, avocado slices, diced tomatoes, corn kernels, chopped cilantro, beans, and a squeeze of lemon juice onto the leaf.
7. Roll the collard leaf, tucking in the sides as you go, to form a burrito-like wrap. Repeat this process with the remaining collard leaves and filling.
8. Serve the Collard Wrap Burritos as a nutritious and flavorful meal.

Cheese Steak Stuffed Bell Peppers

Ingredients:

- 1 onion (chopped)
- Kosher salt
- Parsley (chopped)
- 8 halved bell peppers
- 1 tablespoon of olive oil
- 1 lb. of sirloin steak (chopped)
- 16 oz. of mushrooms
- 16 slices of provol2 cheese
- 2 teaspoons of Italian seasoning
- Black pepper powder

Directions:

1. Preheat the oven to 325°F (165°C).
2. Place the bell peppers in a baking pan and bake for 30 minutes, or until they are slightly tender. Set aside.
3. Heat olive oil in a pan over medium heat.
4. Add the sliced onion, mushrooms, salt, and black pepper to the pan. Cook for about 6 minutes, or until the onions and mushrooms are softened and lightly browned.
5. Add the thinly sliced steak to the pan and season with a bit more salt and pepper. Sauté until the steak is cooked to your desired level of d2ness.
6. Sprinkle the steak mixture with Italian seasoning, and stir to combine the flavors. Cook for an additional 2-3 minutes.
7. Remove the bell peppers from the oven. Place a slice of provol2 cheese at the bottom of each bell pepper cavity.

8. Fill the cavities of the bell peppers with the cooked steak and vegetable mixture.
9. Return the filled bell peppers to the oven and bake for an additional 3 minutes, or until the cheese is melted and bubbly, and the tops of the peppers are golden brown.
10. Remove from the oven and garnish with fresh chopped parsley.
11. Serve the Cheese steak Stuffed Bell Peppers as a delicious and satisfying meal.

Crumbed Asparagus

Ingredients:

- 1 egg
- 2 tbsp plain flour
- 1 cup fresh breadcrumbs, finely chopped
- 1 bunch asparagus, trimmed, cut in half crossways
- Peanut oil, to fry
- Aioli, to serve

Directions:

1. Lightly whisk egg in a bowl.
2. Place plain flour in a separate bowl. Place 1 cup fine fresh breadcrumbs in another bowl.
3. Heat enough peanut oil to come one-third up the side of the wok.

4. Dust the asparagus pieces with flour. Dip in the egg and then the crumbs, pressing down firmly. Cook in batches for 1-2 minutes or until golden. Serve with aioli.

Air Fryer Vegetarian Pumpkin Schnitzel

Ingredients:

- 1/4 cup finely grated cheddar
- 2 tbsp finely chopped hazelnuts
- 1 tbsp finely chopped flat-leaf parsley, plus extra to serve
- 500g butternut pumpkin, peeled
- 1 egg
- 500g potatoes, peeled, cut into 3-4cm pieces
- 250g swede or turnip, peeled, cut into 3-4cm pieces
- 2 1/2 tbsp extra virgin olive oil
- 1/2 cup Panko breadcrumbs

- Lemon wedges, to serve

Directions:

1. Place potatoes and turnip in a medium saucepan and cover with water. Season with salt.
2. Bring to the boil over high heat. Gently boil, covered, for 15 minutes or until tender.
3. Drain well and return to pan. Add 2 tablespoons oil and mash until smooth. Season with salt and pepper.
4. Meanwhile, Preheat Philips Airfryer to 180C.
5. Combine breadcrumbs, cheddar, hazelnuts, parsley and remaining oil in a shallow dish. Season with salt and pepper.
6. Cut pumpkin into 1cm thick slices. Lightly beat egg on a shallow plate.
7. Dip pumpkin into egg to cover all over. Press into breadcrumb mixture to coat all over.
8. Place in the basket, using the grill separator to arrange a second layer of pumpkin. Insert

basket into Airfryer. Cook for 12 minutes or until golden and tender.
9. Serve pumpkin schnitzels with mash and lemon wedges. Sprinkle with extra chopped parsley.

Greek Style Air Fryer Shrimp Skewers

Ingredients:

- 1 tablespoon lemon juice
- 1 teaspoon dried oregano
- 1 teaspoon minced garlic
- Salt and pepper, to taste
- Wooden skewers, soaked in water
- 1 pound shrimp, peeled and deveined
- 2 tablespoons olive oil
- Chopped fresh parsley, for garnish

Directions:

1. Preheat the air fryer to 400°F (200°C).

2. In a bowl, combine the olive oil, lemon juice, dried oregano, minced garlic, salt, and pepper.
3. Thread the shrimp onto the soaked wooden skewers.
4. Brush the shrimp skewers with the marinade, making sure they are coated evenly.
5. Place the shrimp skewers in the air fryer basket.
6. Cook for 5-7 minutes, flipping the skewers halfway through cooking, until the shrimp are pink and cooked through.
7. Remove from the air fryer and garnish with chopped fresh parsley.
8. Serve hot as a flavorful appetizer or main dish.

Crispy Buffalo Tofu Bites

Ingredients:

- 2 tablespoons whole wheat flour
- 1 teaspoon garlic powder
- 1/2 teaspoon onion powder
- Salt and pepper, to taste
- Ranch dressing or blue cheese dressing, for dipping (optional)
- 1 (14-ounce) block of tofu, pressed and cut into cubes
- 2 tablespoons olive oil
- 1/4 cup hot sauce
- Chopped fresh cilantro, for garnish

Directions:

1. Preheat the air fryer to 400°F (200°C).
2. In a bowl, toss the tofu cubes with olive oil, hot sauce, whole wheat flour, garlic powder, onion powder, salt, and pepper until coated evenly.
3. Place the coated tofu cubes in the air fryer basket in a single layer.
4. Cook for 15-20 minutes, shaking the basket occasionally, until the tofu is crispy and golden brown.
5. Remove from the air fryer and let cool for a few minutes.
6. Serve the crispy buffalo tofu bites with ranch dressing or blue cheese dressing for dipping, if desired.
7. Garnish with chopped fresh cilantro.

Cheesy Chicken Bake With Zucchini

Ingredients:

- 2 tsp Italian seasoning
- ½ tsp salt
- ½ tsp black pepper
- 8 oz cream cheese, softened
- ½ cup mayonnaise
- 2 tbsp Worcestershire sauce (sugar-free)
- 2 lb chicken breasts, cubed
- 1 tbsp butter
- 1 cup green bell peppers, sliced
- 1 cup yellow onions, sliced
- 1 zucchini, sliced
- 2 garlic cloves, divided

- 2 cups cheddar cheese, shredded

Directions:

1. Set oven to 370ºF and grease and line a baking dish.
2. Set a pan over medium-high heat. Place in the butter and let melt, then add in the chicken.
3. Cook until browned. Place in onions, zucchini, black pepper, garlic, peppers, salt, and 1 tsp of Italian seasonings. Cook until tender. Set aside.
4. In a bowl, mix cream cheese, garlic, cheddar cheese, remaining seasoning, mayonnaise, and Worcestershire sauce.
5. Stir in meat. Place the mixture into the prepared baking dish then set into the oven. Cook until browned for 30 minutes.

Bacon Chicken Alfredo

Ingredients:

- 1 jar Classico creamy alfredo sauce
- 6 slices chopped hickory bacon
- 4 b2less skinless chicken breasts thawed or fresh
- Pepper and salt to taste
- 4-ounces mushrooms drained and sliced
- 1 cup shredded mozzarella cheese
- ½ cup water

Directions:

1. Add all ingredients in a pot on high fire and bring it to a boil.

2. Once boiling, lower fire to a simmer and cook for 30 minutes, stirring every now and then.
3. Adjust seasoning to taste.
4. Serve and enjoy.

Zucchini Noodle Bowl With Turkey Meatballs

Ingredients:

- 1/4 cup Italian-style bread crumbs
- 1 egg
- 1 teaspoon Italian seasoning
- Salt and pepper to taste
- 2 zucchinis, spiralizer
- 1 tablespoon olive oil
- 1 lb. lean ground turkey
- 1/4 cup marinara sauce

Directions:

1. Heat the olive oil in a large skillet over medium-high heat.

2. In a medium bowl, combine the ground turkey, bread crumbs, egg, Italian seasoning, salt, and pepper. Mix until fully combined and shape into 1-inch meatballs.
3. Add the meatballs to the skillet and cook for 4 to 5 minutes per side, or until cooked through.
4. Add the spiralizer zucchini noodles and marinara sauce to the skillet and stir to combine. Cook for an additional 3 to 4 minutes, or until the zucchini noodles are tender.
5. Serve immediately.

Grilled Shrimp And Avocado Salad

Ingredients:

- 2 cloves garlic, minced

- 2 tablespoons cilantro, chopped
- Salt and pepper to taste
- 4 cups mixed greens
- 1 lb. large shrimp, peeled and deveined
- 2 tablespoons olive oil
- 2 tablespoons freshly squeezed lime juice
- 1 avocado, diced

Directions:

1. In a medium bowl, combine the shrimp, olive oil, lime juice, garlic, cilantro, salt, and pepper. Toss to combine and let marinate for 10 minutes.
2. Preheat the grill to medium-high heat.
3. Thread the shrimp onto skewers and grill for 2 to 3 minutes per side, or until the shrimp are cooked through.

4. In a large bowl, combine the mixed greens and avocado. Slice the shrimp off the skewers and add to the bowl. Drizzle with the remaining marinade and toss to combine.
5. Serve immediately.

Slow Cooker Chicken Tikka Masala

Ingredients:

- 1 tablespoon ground cumin
- 1 tablespoon ground coriander
- 1 teaspoon ground turmeric
- 1/2 teaspoon cayenne pepper
- 2 lbs. b2less, skinless chicken breasts
- 1 onion, chopped
- 2 cloves garlic, minced
- 1 (14.5 oz.) can crushed tomatoes
- 1 tablespoon gram masala
- Salt and pepper to taste

Directions:

1. Add the chicken, onion, garlic, tomatoes, gram masala, cumin, coriander, turmeric, cayenne pepper, salt, and pepper to a slow cooker. Stir to combine.
2. Cover and cook on low for 6 to 8 hours, or until the chicken is cooked through.
3. Serve over cooked cauliflower rice.

Portobello Mushroom Burgers With Avocado

Ingredients:

- Two cloves garlic, minced
- Salt and pepper to taste
- Four whole-grain burger buns
- 2 avocado, sliced
- 4 large portobello mushroom caps
- 1/4 cup of balsamic vinegar
- 2 tbsp. soy sauce
- 2 tbsp. olive oil
- Lettuce, tomato, and onion for garnish

Directions:

1. Combine the balsamic vinegar, soy sauce, olive oil, garlic powder, salt, and pepper in a mixing bowl.
2. After cleaning, take the stems from the portobello mushroom caps.
3. Transfer the mushroom caps to a shallow dish and coat them with the marinade. For a minimum of half an hour, rotating once, let them marinade.
4. Set the grill or pan over medium-high heat to get it hot.
5. To achieve tenderness and attractive grill marks, cook the mushrooms in the marinade for 7 to 10 minutes on each side.
6. Grill the burger buns until they're lightly toasted, perhaps a minute or two.
7. Burgers should be topped with grilled portobello mushrooms, avocado slices, and any other condiments you choose.

8. Here are some Portobello Mushroom Burgers for you to enjoy!

Grilled Eggplant Steaks With Chimichurri

Ingredients:

- Two large eggplants sliced into steaks
- 2 tbsp. olive oil
- Salt and pepper to taste

For chimichurri:

- 1/2 cup of olive oil
- 2 tbsp. red wine vinegar
- 1 tsp dried oregano
- Salt and pepper to taste
- 1 cup of fresh parsley, chopped
- 1/4 cup of fresh cilantro, chopped
- Three cloves garlic, minced

Directions:

1. Set the grill or pan over medium-high heat to get it hot.
2. Add salt and pepper to eggplant steaks before brushing them with olive oil.
3. Cook the eggplant for four to five minutes on each side or until it reaches a soft texture.
4. A bowl containing chopped garlic, parsley, cilantro, olive oil, red wine vinegar, oregano, salt, and pepper is all you need to make chimichurri.
5. Grill the eggplant steaks and then serve with a spoonful of chimichurri.

Zucchini Noodles In Vegan Alfredo Sauce

Ingredients:

- Two cloves garlic, minced
- Juice of 1 lemon

- 1/4 cup of nutritional yeast

- Salt and pepper to taste

- 4 medium zucchinis, spiralized into noodles

- 1 cup of cashews, soaked in water for at least 2 hours

- 1 cup of water

- Fresh parsley for garnish

Directions:

1. The Alfredo sauce is made by blending soaked cashews, water, diced garlic, lemon juice, nutritional yeast, salt, and pepper until smooth.
2. Bring the Alfredo sauce to a simmer in a skillet and set aside to reheat.
3. After coating the noodles with sauce, toss in the zucchini.

4. If you want perfectly cooked noodles, cook them for three to five minutes.
5. Before serving, top with fresh parsley.

Artichoke Hearts Stuffed With Goat Cheese

Ingredients:

- 100 g of goat cheese //- Fresh parsley, chopped //- Grated lemon zest //- Salt and pepper //- 4 pre-cooked artichoke hearts //- Extra virgin olive oil.

Directions:

1. In a bowl, mix the goat cheese with the chopped fresh parsley, the grated lemon zest, salt and pepper.
2. Slightly cut off the tops of the artichoke hearts to create a small cavity.

3. Fill each artichoke heart with the goat cheese mixture.
4. Heat a nonstick skillet over medium heat.
5. Add some olive oil and place the stuffed artichoke hearts in the pan.
6. Cook for a few minutes, turning them gently, until heated through and lightly browned.
7. Arrange the stuffed artichoke hearts on a serving plate.
8. You can garnish with some extra chopped fresh parsley.
9. Serve artichoke hearts as an elegant and flavorful appetizer, suitable for the ketogenic diet.
10. These goat cheese stuffed artichoke hearts offer a combination of delicate and creamy flavors.
11. The goat cheese gives it a velvety texture and a unique flavor, while the parsley and lemon zest add freshness and aroma. The olive oil

contributes a touch of richness and depth of flavour.

Eggs Stuffed With Guacamole

Ingredients:

- Fresh chile pepper or cayenne pepper, minced (optional, for a spicy twist)

- Salt and pepper

- Cherry tomatoes, halved, for garnish

- 6 boiled eggs

- 2 ripe avocados

- lime juice

- Fresh cilantro, chopped, for garnish (optional).

Directions:

1. Peel the hard-boiled eggs and cut them in half lengthwise.
2. Remove the yolks and place them in a bowl.
3. Mash the yolks with a fork until you get a fine consistency.
4. Preparation for the guacamole:
5. In a bowl, mash ripe avocados until smooth.
6. Add the lime juice, crushed red pepper (if desired), salt and pepper. Mix well.
7. Add the mashed egg yolks to the bowl with the guacamole and mix until creamy.
8. Fill the hard-boiled egg halves with the egg-guacamole mixture.
9. Place the halved cherry tomatoes on top of each stuffed egg.
10. You can garnish with some freshly chopped coriander for a pop of color and freshness.
11. Arrange the guacamole-filled eggs on a serving plate.

12. Serve as a fresh and colorful appetizer, perfect for the ketogenic diet.
13. These guacamole stuffed eggs are a delicious combination of creaminess and freshness.
14. The guacamole offers a rich flavor from the avocado and a hint of tartness from the lime.
15. The addition of the cherry tomatoes adds a touch of sweetness and the fresh coriander gives it a fresh and aromatic flavour.

Green Olives Stuffed With Cream Cheese

Ingredients:

- Grated lemon zest
- Fresh parsley, chopped
- Black pepper
- 20 pitted green olives
- 50 g of cream cheese (philadelphia type)
- Extra virgin olive oil.

Directions:

1. In a bowl, mix the cream cheese with the grated lemon zest, the chopped fresh parsley and a light grind of black pepper.
2. Using a small teaspoon, fill each green olive with a small amount of the prepared cream cheese.

3. Arrange the stuffed green olives on a serving plate.
4. You can add a splash of extra virgin olive oil on top of the stuffed olives for an extra kick of flavor.
5. Serve green olives stuffed with cream cheese as an irresistible and rich appetizer, perfect for the ketogenic diet.
6. These cream cheese stuffed green olives offer a balanced flavor combination. The pitted green olives give it a salty and slightly bitter taste, while the cream cheese gives it softness and a touch of delicate flavour.
7. Grated lemon zest and fresh parsley complete the dish with fresh and aromatic notes.

Spicy Cajun Seafood Jambalaya Recipe

Ingredients:

- 12 ounces smoked sausage, sliced

- 1 can (14.5 oz) diced tomatoes

- 1 cup long-grain white rice and 2 cups chicken or seafood broth

- 2 tablespoons Cajun seasoning

- 1 teaspoon dried thyme, 1 teaspoon paprika, salt and black pepper

- 1/2 teaspoon cayenne pepper (adjust to taste)

- 1 tablespoon vegetable oil

- 1 onion, diced, and 3 cloves garlic, minced

- 1 green bell pepper diced, and 2 celery stalks, diced

- 1 pound shrimp, peeled and deveined

- 1 pound crawfish tails (or substitute with crab meat)

- Fresh parsley for garnish and lemon wedges for serving

Directions:

1. Heat the vegetable oil in a large pot or oven over medium heat.
2. Add the diced onion, green bell pepper, celery, and minced garlic to the pot. Sauté for 5 minutes until the vegetables are softened.
3. Stir in the sliced smoked sausage and cook until slightly browned.
4. Add the shrimp and crawfish tails to the pot and cook for 2-3 minutes until they turn pink and opaque.
5. Stir in the diced tomatoes, long-grain rice, chicken or seafood broth, Cajun seasoning, dried thyme, paprika, cayenne pepper, salt, and black pepper.
6. Bring the mixture to a boil, then reduce the heat to low. Cover the pot and let it simmer

for about 20-25 minutes until the rice is cooked and the flavors have melded together.
7. Remove from heat and let the jambalaya sit, covered, for 5 minutes.
8. Garnish with fresh parsley and serve with lemon wedges.

Moroccan Seafood Paella With Saffron Rice Recipe

Ingredients:

- 1 red bell pepper, diced, and 1 cup cherry tomatoes, halved
- ½ cup frozen peas
- 2 tablespoons olive oil
- 1 teaspoon ground cumin and ½ teaspoon turmeric
- ½ teaspoon smoked paprika
- A pinch of saffron threads (soaked in 2 tablespoons of warm water)
- Salt and pepper to taste

- 1 lb mixed seafood (shrimp, mussels, calamari)

- 1 ½ cups Arborio rice

- 3 ½ cups fish or vegetable broth

- 1 onion, finely chopped, and 3 garlic cloves, minced

- Lemon wedges and fresh parsley for garnish

Directions:

1. Heat olive oil over medium heat in a large paella pan or skillet. Sauté onions and garlic until softened.
2. Add the red bell pepper, cumin, smoked paprika, turmeric, saffron (with water), salt, and pepper. Cook for a few minutes until fragrant.
3. Stir in Arborio rice and coat it with the spices. Pour in the broth and bring to a simmer.

4. Add the mixed seafood, cherry tomatoes, and frozen peas. Gently stir to distribute the ingredients evenly.
5. Cover the pan and let it simmer for about 20 minutes until the rice is cooked and the seafood is tender.
6. Once d2, please remove it from the heat and let it rest for a few minutes.
7. Garnish with lemon wedges and fresh parsley before serving.

Baked Salmon With Roasted Vegetables

Ingredients:

- Bell peppers, sliced
- Olive oil
- Garlic powder
- Paprika
- 4 oz salmon filet
- Broccoli florets
- Cauliflower florets
- Salt and pepper to taste

Directions:

1. Preheat the oven to 400°F (200°C).
2. Spot the salmon filet on a baking sheet lined with parchment paper.

3. Arrange the broccoli florets, cauliflower florets, and bell peppers around the salmon.
4. Drizzle olive oil over the salmon and vegetables. Spray it with garlic powder, paprika, salt, and pepper.
5. Bake for fifteen to twenty minutes or until the salmon is boiled through and the vegetables are tender.
6. Serve hot.

Vegetable Stir-Fry With Tofu

Ingredients:

- Carrot, julienned

- Snow peas

- Low-sodium soy sauce

- Garlic, minced

- Ginger, grated

- 4 oz tofu, cubed

- Broccoli florets

- Bell peppers, sliced

- Olive oil

Directions:

1. Heat olive oil in a big pan or wok over medium-high warmth.
2. Put in the tofu cubes and cook until golden brown. Extract from the pan and set aside.
3. In the same pan, add the broccoli florets, bell peppers, carrot, snow peas, minced garlic, and grated ginger.
4. Stir-fry for a few minutes until the vegetables are tender-crisp.
5. Return the toftofu toe skillet and drizzle with low-sodium soy sauce. Stir well to combine.
6. Cook for an additional minute, then remove from heat.
7. Serve hot.

Chicken Enchilada

Ingredients:

- 2 cups of Monterey Jack cheese (shredded)
- ½ pc of onion (chopped)
- 1 bell pepper (chopped)
- 1 teaspoon of cumin
- 2 cloves of garlic (diced)
- Kosher salt
- 1 tablespoon of olive oil
- 12 pcs of tortillas
- 2 cups of cheddar cheese (shredded)
- 10 oz. of enchilada sauce
- 8 oz of tomatoes (squashed)

- 3 cups of chicken (thinly sliced)

- ¼ cup of cilantro (chopped)

Directions:

1. Preheat the oven to 350°F (175°C).
2. Heat oil in a pan over medium heat.
3. Once the oil is heated up, add the diced onion and bell pepper. Cook for about 5 minutes, until they become softened and lightly browned.
4. Add cumin and minced garlic to the pan and sauté for 1 minute, until fragrant.
5. Stir in the diced tomatoes and enchilada sauce. Let the mixture simmer for about 5 minutes, allowing the flavors to meld together. Set aside 1 ½ cups of the sauce for later use.
6. In a bowl, combine 1 cup of shredded Monterey Jack cheese, shredded chicken, 1 cup of shredded cheddar cheese, chopped

cilantro, 1 cup of the sauce (from step 5), and salt. Mix well to combine.
7. Place 2 tortilla on a clean surface or chopping board. Spoon a portion of the chicken mixture onto the center of the tortilla, then roll it up tightly. Place the rolled enchilada seam-side down in a baking dish.
8. Repeat the process with the remaining tortillas and chicken mixture, arranging them side by side in the baking dish.
9. Drizzle ½ cup of the reserved enchilada sauce over the enchiladas, and sprinkle another cup of shredded Monterey Jack and cheddar cheese on top.
10. Bake the enchiladas in the preheated oven for about 10 minutes, or until the cheese is melted and bubbly.
11. Serve the chicken enchiladas hot, garnished with fresh cilantro.

Zucchini Chips

Ingredients:

- 50g (1/4 cup) semolina
- 20g (1/4 cup) finely grated parmesan
- 1 1/2 tbsp finely chopped fresh thyme
- 1/2 tsp garlic powder
- 1 lemon, rind finely grated
- 4 zucchini
- 1/2 tsp fine salt
- 40g (1/3 cup) almond meal
- 1 egg, whisked

Directions:

1. Preheat oven to 220C/200C fan-forced. Line a large baking tray with baking paper. Cut zucchini on the diagonal into 1cm thick slices, then cut into 1cm batons (about 3 batons per slice).
2. Place zucchini batons in a colander set over a bowl. Sprinkle with salt and toss to coat. Set aside for 10 minutes to drain.
3. Combine almond meal, semolina, parmesan, thyme, garlic powder and lemon rind in a bowl.
4. Pat zucchini dry with paper towel. Place the egg in a shallow bowl. Working in batches, dip zucchini batons in egg, draining off excess.
5. Toss in semolina mixture, to coat. Place, in a single layer, on the prepared tray.
6. Spray well with olive oil and bake, turning chips every 10 minutes, for 25-30 minutes or until golden and crisp. Season with sea salt and serve immediately.

Cinnamon Nut Scrolls

Ingredients:

- 1 egg
- 2/3 cup finely chopped walnuts
- 1/3 cup slivered almonds, toasted
- 1/4 cup brown sugar
- 1 tsp ground cinnamon
- 2 tbsp golden syrup
- 2 1/4 cups self-raising flour
- 1 tbsp caster sugar
- 100g butter, chilled, finely chopped
- 2/3 cup milk

Directions:

1. Preheat oven to 200°C/180°C fan-forced. Grease a 3cm-deep, 19cm x 29cm (base) slice pan.
2. Combine flour and caster sugar in a bowl. Rub in half the butter until mixture resembles coarse breadcrumbs.
3. Combine milk and egg in a jug. Stir into flour mixture until soft, sticky dough forms. Turn out onto a lightly floured surface. Knead for 30 seconds or until smooth.
4. Roll dough out to a 30cm x 40cm rectangle. Sprinkle with walnuts and almonds. Top with brown sugar and cinnamon. Dot with remaining butter.
5. Roll up dough tightly from one long side. Using a serrated knife, trim ends. Cut roll into 12 slices.
6. Place slices in prepared pan. Bake for 22 to 25 minutes or until golden. Serve scrolls warm with golden syrup.

Gluten-Free Salt And Pepper Tofu

Ingredients:

- 1/2 cup (125ml) salt-reduced gluten-free tamari or soy sauce
- 1/4 cup (55g) caster sugar
- 1 tsp sesame oil
- 1 tbsp sea salt flakes
- 1 tbsp black peppercorns
- 1 tsp dried chilli flakes (optional)
- 1/4 cup (45g) rice flour
- 2 x 300g pkts firm tofu, cut into 2cm pieces
- 4 Method Steps
- 2 tsp vegetable oil

- 1 spring onion, thinly sliced

- 1 long red chilli, thinly sliced (optional)

- 1 garlic clove, crushed

- Vegetable oil, extra, to shallow-fry

Directions:

1. Heat the vegetable oil in a small saucepan over high heat. Add spring onion, sliced chilli, if using, and garlic and cook, stirring, for 1 min or until fragrant. Reduce heat to low.
2. Add the tamari or soy sauce and sugar. Cook, stirring, for 3 mins or until the sugar dissolves. Simmer for 5 mins or until the sauce thickens. Stir in sesame oil.
3. Place the sea salt, peppercorns and chilli flakes, if using, in a mortar and pound with a pestle until finely crushed (alternatively, use a spice grinder). Place in a medium bowl with the rice flour and stir to combine.

4. Add the tofu to the rice flour mixture and toss to coat, shaking off excess.
5. Add enough oil to a medium frying pan to come 1cm up the side. Heat over medium heat.
6. Cook the tofu, in 2 batches, turning occasionally, for 5 mins or until golden brown. Transfer to a plate lined with paper towel.
7. Arrange the tofu on a serving platter. Serve with the sauce.

Ranch Zucchini Fritters

Ingredients:

- 2 tablespoons chopped fresh parsley
- 1 tablespoon dried ranch seasoning mix
- 2 eggs, beaten
- Salt and pepper, to taste
- 2 medium zucchinis, grated
- 1/4 cup whole wheat flour
- 1/4 cup grated Parmesan cheese
- Olive oil spray

Directions:

1. Preheat the air fryer to 375°F (190°C).
2. Place the grated zucchinis in a colander and sprinkle with salt. Let sit for 10 minutes to

release excess moisture. Squeeze out any remaining liquid from the zucchinis.
3. In a bowl, combine the grated zucchinis, whole wheat flour, grated Parmesan cheese, chopped fresh parsley, dried ranch seasoning mix, beaten eggs, salt, and pepper. Mix well to form a batter.
4. Scoop spoonfuls of the zucchini batter and shape them into fritters.
5. Lightly spray the air fryer basket with olive oil.
6. Place the zucchini fritters in the air fryer basket in a single layer.
7. Cook for 10-12 minutes, flipping the fritters halfway through cooking, until they are golden brown and crispy.
8. Remove from the air fryer and let cool slightly before serving.

Lemon Herb Air Fryer Tilapia

Ingredients:

- 1 teaspoon dried parsley
- 1/2 teaspoon dried dill
- 1/2 teaspoon dried thyme
- 1/2 teaspoon garlic powder
- Salt and pepper, to taste
- Lemon wedges, for serving
- 4 tilapia fillets
- 2 tablespoons olive oil
- 2 tablespoons lemon juice
- Chopped fresh parsley, for garnish

Directions:

1. Preheat the air fryer to 400°F (200°C).
2. In a bowl, whisk together the olive oil, lemon juice, dried parsley, dried dill, dried thyme, garlic powder, salt, and pepper.
3. Place the tilapia fillets in the bowl and turn them to coat them in the marinade.
4. Place the marinated tilapia fillets in the air fryer basket.
5. Cook for 8-10 minutes, until the tilapia is opaque and flakes easily with a fork.
6. Squeeze lemon wedges over the tilapia fillets.
7. Garnish with chopped fresh parsley and serve hot.

Mediterranean Eggplant Dip

Ingredients:

- 2 cloves garlic, minced
- 1 tablespoon olive oil

- 1/2 teaspoon ground cumin
- Salt and pepper, to taste
- 1 large eggplant
- 1/4 cup tahini
- 2 tablespoons lemon juice
- Chopped fresh parsley, for garnish

Directions:

1. Preheat the air fryer to 400°F (200°C).
2. Pierce the eggplant with a fork in several places.
3. Place the eggplant in the air fryer basket.
4. Cook for 25-30 minutes, until the eggplant is soft and the skin is charred.
5. Remove the eggplant from the air fryer and let cool slightly.
6. Cut the eggplant in half lengthwise and scoop out the flesh into a bowl.

7. Add the tahini, lemon juice, minced garlic, olive oil, ground cumin, salt, and pepper to the bowl with the eggplant flesh.
8. Use a fork or a blender to mash or blend the ingredients together until smooth and well combined.
9. Garnish with chopped fresh parsley before serving.
10. Serve the baba ghanoush with pita bread, fresh vegetables, or as a spread.

Thyme Chicken Thighs

Ingredients:

- ½ cup chopped onion
- 4 chicken thighs
- ¼ cup heavy cream
- 2 tbsp Dijon mustard
- 1 tsp thyme
- ½ cup chicken stock
- 1 tbsp olive oil
- 1 tsp garlic powder

Directions:

1. Heat the olive oil in a pan. Cook the chicken for about 4 minutes per side. Set aside.

2. Sauté the onion in the same pan for 3 minutes, add the stock, and simmer for 5 minutes.
3. Stir in mustard and heavy cream, along with thyme and garlic powder. Pour the sauce over the chicken and serve.

Garlic & Ginger Chicken With Peanut Sauce

Ingredients:

- 1 tsp minced garlic
- 1 tsp minced ginger
- 1 tbsp olive oil
- 1 tbsp rice wine vinegar
- 1 tsp cayenne pepper
- 1 tsp erythritol
- 6 chicken thighs
- 1 tbsp wheat-free soy sauce
- 1 tbsp sugar-free fish sauce
- 1 tbsp lime juice
- 1 tsp cilantro

Sauce:

- 1 tsp minced ginger
- 1 tbsp chopped jalapeño
- 2 tbsp rice wine vinegar
- 2 tbsp erythritol
- 1 tbsp fish sauce
- ½ cup peanut butter
- 1 tsp minced garlic
- 1 tbsp lime juice
- 2 tbsp water

Directions:

1. Combine all chicken ingredients in a large Ziploc bag. Seal the bag and shake to combine.

2. Refrigerate for 1 hour. Remove from fridge about 15 minutes before cooking.
3. Preheat the grill to medium and grill the chicken for 7 minutes per side. Whisk together all sauce ingredients in a mixing bowl. Serve the chicken drizzled with peanut sauce.

Pork Chops With Cranberry Sauce

Ingredients:

- 1 14-ounce fresh cranberries, pitted
- 5 tablespoons butter
- Salt and pepper to taste
- 6-pieces b2-in pork loin chops
- 1 cup water

Directions:

1. Add all ingredients in a pot on high fire and bring to a boil.
2. Once boiling, lower fire to a simmer and cook for 25 minutes.
3. Adjust seasoning to taste.
4. Serve and enjoy.

Turkey Burgers With Avocado

Ingredients:

- 2 cloves garlic, minced
- 2 tablespoons cilantro, chopped
- Salt and pepper to taste
- 4 lettuce leaves
- 1 lb. lean ground turkey
- 2 tablespoons freshly squeezed lime juice
- 1 avocado, sliced

Directions:

1. In a medium bowl, combine the ground turkey, lime juice, garlic, cilantro, salt, and pepper. Form into 4 equal-sized patties.

2. Heat a large skillet over medium-high heat. Add the turkey burgers and cook for 4 to 5 minutes per side, or until cooked through.
3. Serve the burgers on lettuce leaves topped with sliced avocado.

Greek Yogurt Chicken Salad

Ingredients:

- 2 tablespoons fresh parsley, chopped
- Salt and pepper to taste
- 2 cups plain Greek yogurt
- 2 tablespoons Dijon mustard
- 2 tablespoons h2y
- 2 b2less, skinless chicken breasts
- 2 tablespoons olive oil
- 2 cloves garlic, minced
- 2 tablespoons fresh lemon juice
- 1/4 cup crumbled feta cheese

Directions:

1. Preheat the oven to 400°F.
2. In a small bowl, combine the olive oil, garlic, lemon juice, parsley, salt, and pepper. Brush the mixture over the chicken breasts.
3. Place the chicken on a parchment-lined baking sheet and bake for 12 to 15 minutes, or until the chicken is cooked through. Let cool.
4. In a separate bowl, combine the Greek yogurt, Dijon mustard, h2y, and feta cheese.
5. Shred the cooled chicken and add to the yogurt mixture. Stir to combine.
6. Serve over a bed of mixed greens.

Baked Halibut With Spinach And Tomatoes

Ingredients:

- 2 tablespoons fresh lemon juice
- 2 tablespoons fresh parsley, chopped
- Salt and pepper to taste
- 2 cups baby spinach
- 4 (4-ounce) halibut fillets
- 2 tablespoons olive oil
- 2 cloves garlic, minced
- 1 cup cherry tomatoes, halved

Directions:

1. Preheat the oven to 400°F.

2. In a small bowl, combine the olive oil, garlic, lemon juice, parsley, salt, and pepper. Brush the mixture over the halibut fillets.
3. Arrange the spinach and tomatoes in the bottom of a baking dish. Place the halibut fillets on top.
4. Bake for 12 to 15 minutes, or until the halibut is cooked through and flakes easily. Serve immediately.

Coconut Curry Cauliflower Soup

Ingredients:

- 1 tbsp. curry powder

- 1 tsp turmeric

- 4 cups of vegetable broth

- Salt and pepper to taste

- Fresh cilantro for garnish

- Lime wedges for serving
- 2 medium cauliflower, chopped
- 2 can (400ml) coconut milk
- 2 onion, chopped
- Two cloves garlic, minced

Directions:

1. To soften the onion and garlic, sauté them in a big saucepan.
2. Finish cooking for 5 minutes after adding turmeric, curry powder, and cauliflower.
3. Simmer after adding the coconut milk and veggie broth.
4. Simmer until cauliflower reaches a soft texture, about 20-25 minutes.
5. To make a silky-smooth soup, use an immersion blender.

6. Add salt and pepper according to your preference.
7. Serve with slices of lime and top with chopped fresh cilantro.

Green Beans With Toasted Almonds And Lemon

Ingredients:

- 1/2 cup of sliced almonds
- 2 tbsp. olive oil
- 2 lemon, zest and juice
- 1 lb green beans, trimmed
- Salt and pepper to taste

Directions:

1. Blanch or steam green beans for three to five minutes or until they are crisp-tender.
2. Slice the almonds and toast them in a skillet over medium heat until golden.
3. In the same skillet, heat the olive oil and toss in the blanched green beans.

4. Add the toasted almonds, lemon zest, and lemon juice to the green beans and toss to combine.
5. Add salt and pepper according to your preference.

Mashed Cauliflower With Garlic And Herbs

Ingredients:

- 2 tbsp. olive oil
- 1/4 cup of almond milk (or any non-dairy milk)
- 2 tbsp. nutritional yeast
- Salt and pepper to taste
- 2 large head of cauliflower, cut into florets
- Two cloves garlic, minced
- Fresh herbs (e.g., chives, parsley) for garnish

Directions:

1. Get the cauliflower florets incredibly soft by steaming or boiling them.
2. Be sure to mince the garlic before adding the cauliflower, olive oil, almond milk, and

nutritional yeast to a blender or food processor.
3. To get a smooth mixture, blend with more almond milk as required.
4. Add salt and pepper according to your preference.
5. Add some fresh herbs as a garnish just before serving.

Roast Chicken With Avocado Salsa

Ingredients:

- 4 chicken breasts
- Extra virgin olive oil
- Salt and pepper.

Avocado salsa ingredients:

- lime juice
- minced garlic
- Fresh parsley, chopped
- 2 ripe avocados
- Salt and pepper.

Directions:

1. Preheat the oven to 180°C.

2. Drizzle the chicken breasts with a drizzle of olive oil, salt, and pepper.
3. Arrange the chicken breasts on a baking sheet and bake in the preheated oven for about 20-25 minutes or until cooked through and succulent.
4. Preparation for Avocado Dip:
5. In a bowl, mash ripe avocados until smooth.
6. Add the lime juice, minced garlic, chopped fresh parsley, salt and pepper. Mix well.
7. Arrange the roasted chicken breasts on a serving platter.
8. Pour the avocado salsa over the chicken breasts or serve it on the side as a condiment.
9. Serve Roasted Chicken with Avocado Salsa as a tasty and healthy appetizer, suitable for the ketogenic diet.
10. This Roasted Chicken with Avocado Salsa is a great appetizer option on the ketogenic diet. The roasted chicken offers a source of lean

protein, while the avocado dip adds a creamy, crisp note. The garlic and parsley impart tasty aromas that pair perfectly with the flavor of the chicken.

Ham And Rocket Leaves

Ingredients:

- Extra virgin olive oil
- Lemon juice
- Parmesan cheese flakes (optional)
- 100 g of raw ham
- 1 bunch of fresh rocket
- Salt and pepper.

Directions:

1. Wash and dry the rocket, then roughly chop it.
2. Spread a slice of raw ham on a flat surface.
3. Arrange a small amount of rocket on the prosciutto slice.
4. Rolling up:

5. Roll up the slice of ham with the rocket inside, creating a small sheet.
6. Repeat the process with the other slices of ham.
7. In a bowl, mix a little extra virgin olive oil, lemon juice, salt and pepper.
8. Lightly season the ham and rocket leaves with the prepared sauce.
9. Arrange the ham and rocket leaves on a serving plate.
10. You can add a few shavings of Parmesan cheese on top of the pastry for an extra touch of flavor.
11. Serve the puff pastries as a light and tasty appetizer, perfect for the ketogenic diet.
12. These Prosciutto and Arugula Puff Pastries are a simple and flavorful appetizer option on the ketogenic diet.

13. The raw ham offers a rich, salty flavor, while the rocket adds freshness and a slightly bitter edge.
14. The dressing of olive oil and lemon juice completes the dish with a note of acidity and freshness.

Chicken And Vegetable Skewers

Ingredients:

- Red onion, cut into wedges
- Zucchini, cut into rings
- Extra virgin olive oil
- Spices to taste (paprika, oregano, rosemary, etc.)
- 2 chicken breasts, diced
- Bell peppers (various colors), cut into pieces
- Salt and pepper.

Directions:

1. In a bowl, season the chicken cubes with a little olive oil, spices to taste, salt and pepper. Mix well to distribute the spices evenly.

2. Prepare the vegetables cut into pieces.
3. Thread them alternately onto the skewer sticks, alternating between chicken pieces and vegetables.
4. Preheat a grill or nonstick skillet.
5. Brush the grate or pan with a little olive oil to prevent the ingredients from sticking.
6. Cook the chicken and vegetable kebabs, turning occasionally, until the chicken is cooked through and the vegetables are tender and lightly charred.
7. Arrange the chicken and vegetable skewers on a serving platter.
8. You can garnish with some chopped fresh parsley or a drizzle of extra virgin olive oil.
9. Serve the kebabs as a tasty and colorful appetizer, perfect for the ketogenic diet.
10. Chicken and vegetable skewers are a great appetizer option on the ketogenic diet.

Chicken offers lean protein, while vegetables add color, fiber and flavor.
11. The spices and olive oil give depth of flavor and cooking on the grill adds a slight smoky note. A tasty and balanced option to satisfy the palate.

Creamy Lemon Herb Salmon Pasta Recipe

Ingredients:

- 1 cup heavy cream

- 1 cup chicken or vegetable broth

- Zest of 1 lemon, juice of half a lemon

- 1 teaspoon dried basil

- 1 teaspoon dried oregano

- Salt and pepper to taste

- 12 oz fettuccine or your favorite pasta

- 1 lb salmon fillet, skinless and b2less

- 2 tablespoons olive oil

- 4 garlic cloves, minced

- Fresh parsley, chopped, for garnish

Directions:

1. Cook the pasta according to package Directions:until al dente. Drain and set aside.
2. Season the salmon fillet with salt and pepper. Heat olive oil over medium heat in a large skillet and cook the salmon for about 4 minutes per side or until cooked through. Remove the salmon from the pan and flake it into bite-sized pieces.
3. In the same skillet, sauté garlic until fragrant. Pour in the chicken or vegetable broth, heavy cream, lemon zest, lemon juice, basil, and oregano. Bring to a simmer and let the sauce thicken for 5 minutes.
4. Add the flaked salmon to the sauce and stir to combine.
5. Toss the cooked pasta into the creamy salmon sauce until well-coated
6. Season with additional salt and pepper if needed.

7. Garnish with fresh parsley before serving.

Spiced Seafood Fried Rice Recipe

Ingredients:

- 1 red bell pepper, diced
- 1 cup frozen peas
- 2 tablespoons soy sauce and 1 tablespoon fish sauce
- 1 teaspoon ground cumin
- 1/2 teaspoon paprika
- 1/2 teaspoon chili flakes (adjust to taste)
- 1 cup long-grain white rice
- 1 lb mixed seafood (shrimp, squid, and mussels), cleaned
- 2 tablespoons vegetable oil

- 1 onion, finely chopped, and 3 garlic cloves, minced

- 1 carrot, diced

- 2 green onions, sliced, and Sesame seeds for garnish

Directions:

1. Cook the rice according to package Directions:and let it cool.
2. Heat the vegetable oil over medium heat in a large wok or skillet.
3. Add the chopped onion and minced garlic. Sauté until fragrant.
4. Stir in the diced carrot, red bell pepper, and frozen peas. Cook until the vegetables are tender.
5. Push the vegetables to 2 side of the wok and add the mixed seafood. Cook until the seafood is fully cooked.

6. Incorporate the cooled rice into the wok, stirring to combine with the vegetables and seafood.
7. Season with soy sauce, fish sauce, ground cumin, paprika, and chili flakes. Mix well.
8. Garnish with sliced green onions and sesame seeds before serving.

Quinoa Salad With Avocado And Black Beans

Ingredients:

- Avocado, diced
- Red onion, diced
- Cilantro chopped
- Lime juice
- Olive oil
- 1/2 cup cooked quinoa
- 1/4 cup black beans, rinsed and drained
- Cherry tomatoes, halved
- Salt and pepper to taste

Directions:

1. In a bowl, combine the cooked quinoa, black beans, cherry tomatoes, avocado, red onion, and cilantro.
2. Drizzle with lime juice and olive oil.
3. Season with salt and pepper to taste.
4. Toss everything together until well mixed.
5. Serve chilled or at room temperature.

Egg Salad Lettuce Wraps

Ingredients:

- Green onions, chopped
- Greek yogurt (plain, non-fat)
- Dijon mustard
- Lettuce leaves (butter lettuce works well)
- 2 hard-boiled eggs, chopped
- Celery, diced
- Salt and pepper to taste

Directions:

1. In a bowl, combine the chopped hard-boiled eggs, diced celery, and chopped green onions.
2. Add Greek yogurt and Dijon mustard to the bowl and mix well.

3. Season with salt and pepper to taste.
4. Spoon the egg salad onto individual lettuce leaves and wrap them up.
5. Serve chilled.

Lentil Soup

Ingredients:

- Garlic, minced
- Low-sodium vegetable broth
- Ground cumin
- Paprika
- Turmeric
- Salt and pepper to taste
- 1 cup lentils
- Onion, chopped
- Carrot, chopped
- Celery, chopped

Directions:

1. Rinse the lentils under cold water.
2. In a large pot, sauté the chopped onion, carrot, celery, and minced garlic until softened.
3. Add the lentils to the pot and pour in the vegetable broth.
4. Season with ground cumin, paprika, turmeric, salt, and pepper.
5. Bring to a boil, then reduce heat and simmer for about 30 minutes or until the lentils are tender.
6. Serve hot.

Sweet Potato Fries

Ingredients:

- ½ teaspoon salt
- ¼ teaspoon garlic powder
- ¼ teaspoon paprika
- 2 medium sweet potatoes peeled
- 2 teaspoons olive oil
- ⅛ teaspoon black pepper

Directions:

1. Preheat the air fryer to 380°F. Peel the sweet potatoes, then slice each potato into even ¼ inch thick sticks.
2. Place the sweet potatoes in a large mixing bow, and toss with olive oil, salt, garlic powder, paprika and black pepper.

3. Cook in 2 or 3 batches, depending on the size of your basket without overcrowding the pan until they're crispy. I recommend 12 minutes, turning half way. This may vary based on your air fryer.
4. Serve immediately with your favorite dipping sauce.

Air Fryer Butternut Squash

Ingredients:

- 4 cups cubed butternut squash
- 1 tsp ground cinnamon
- Olive oil cooking spray

Directions:

1. Spray the air fryer basket with olive oil cooking spray or line it with foil and spray.
2. Place the butternut squash in the basket.
3. Sprinkle with cinnamon and coat with olive oil spray.
4. Cook at 390 degrees for 20 minutes. It's best to check on it after 10 minutes, stir, coat and continue cooking. At this point, you can also add more cinnamon if you prefer.
5. Serve.

Ginger Soy Air Fryer Beef Stir Fry

Ingredients:

- 1 tablespoon rice vinegar
- 1 tablespoon h2y or maple syrup
- 1 tablespoon grated ginger
- 1 teaspoon minced garlic
- 1 teaspoon cornstarch
- 1 tablespoon water
- 2 cups mixed vegetables (such as bell peppers, broccoli, carrots, snap peas)
- Salt and pepper, to taste
- 1 pound beef sirloin, thinly sliced
- 2 tablespoons low-sodium soy sauce

- Sliced green onions, for garnish

Directions:

1. Preheat the air fryer to 400°F (200°C).
2. In a bowl, combine the soy sauce, rice vinegar, h2y or maple syrup, grated ginger, minced garlic, salt, and pepper.
3. Add the beef sirloin slices to the bowl and toss to coat them in the marinade.
4. In a small bowl, mix the cornstarch and water to create a slurry.
5. Place the marinated beef and mixed vegetables in the air fryer basket.
6. Cook for 8-10 minutes, shaking the basket occasionally, until the beef is cooked to your desired level of d2ness and the vegetables are tender-crisp.
7. Pour the cornstarch slurry over the cooked beef and vegetables, tossing gently to coat and thicken the sauce.

8. Garnish with sliced green onions before serving.
9. Serve the ginger soy beef stir fry over rice or noodles.

Spicy Air Fryer Cauliflower Bites

Ingredients:

- 2 tablespoons hot sauce
- 1 teaspoon paprika
- 1/2 teaspoon garlic powder
- Salt and pepper, to taste
- Ranch or blue cheese dressing, for dipping (optional)
- 1 medium head of cauliflower, cut into florets
- 1/4 cup olive oil
- Chopped fresh parsley, for garnish

Directions:

1. Preheat the air fryer to 400°F (200°C).

2. In a bowl, whisk together the olive oil, hot sauce, paprika, garlic powder, salt, and pepper.
3. Add the cauliflower florets to the bowl and toss to coat them in the spicy mixture.
4. Place the coated cauliflower florets in the air fryer basket in a single layer.
5. Cook for 15-18 minutes, shaking the basket occasionally, until the cauliflower is crispy and lightly browned.
6. Remove from the air fryer and let cool for a few minutes.
7. Serve the spicy cauliflower bites with ranch or blue cheese dressing for dipping, if desired.
8. Garnish with chopped fresh parsley.

Garlic Herb Air Fryer Pork Chops

Ingredients:

- 2 cloves garlic, minced
- 1 tablespoon chopped fresh parsley
- 1 teaspoon dried thyme
- 1/2 teaspoon dried rosemary
- 4 b2less pork chops
- 2 tablespoons olive oil
- Salt and pepper, to taste

Directions:

1. Preheat the air fryer to 400°F (200°C).
2. In a bowl, combine the olive oil, minced garlic, chopped fresh parsley, dried thyme, dried rosemary, salt, and pepper.

3. Rub the pork chops with the mixture, making sure to coat them evenly.
4. Place the pork chops in the air fryer basket.
5. Cook for 10-12 minutes, flipping the chops halfway through cooking, until the pork is cooked through and browned.
6. Remove from the air fryer and let rest for a few minutes.
7. Serve the garlic herb pork chops hot with your favorite side dishes.

Pork Burgers With Caramelized Onion Rings

Ingredients:

- 1 white onion, sliced into rings
- 1 tbsp balsamic vinegar
- 3 drops liquid stevia
- 6 low carb burger buns, halved
- 2 lb ground pork
- Pink salt and chili pepper to taste
- 3 tbsp olive oil
- 1 tbsp butter
- 2 firm tomatoes, sliced into rings

Directions:

1. Combine the pork, salt and chili pepper in a bowl and mold out 6 patties.
2. Heat the olive oil in a skillet over medium heat and fry the patties for 4 to 5 minutes on each side until golden brown on the outside.
3. Remove onto a plate and sit for 3 minutes.
4. Meanwhile, melt butter in a skillet over medium heat, sauté the onions for 2 minutes to be soft, and stir in the balsamic vinegar and liquid stevia.
5. Cook for 30 seconds stirring once or twice until caramelized. In each bun, place a patty, top with some onion rings and 2 tomato rings. Serve the burgers with cheddar cheese dip.

Creamy Pork Chops

Ingredients:

- 1 onion, peeled and chopped
- 1 cup heavy cream
- 3 pork chops, b2less
- 1 tsp ground nutmeg
- ¼ cup coconut oil
- 8 ounces mushrooms, sliced
- 1 tsp garlic powder

Directions:

1. Set a pan over medium heat and warm the oil, add in the onions and mushrooms, and cook for 4 minutes.

2. Stir in the pork chops, season with garlic powder, and nutmeg, and sear until browned.
3. Put the pan in the oven at 350ºF, and bake for 30 minutes.
4. Remove pork chops to bowls and maintain warm. Place the pan over medium heat, pour in the heavy cream and vinegar over the mushrooms mixture, and cook for 5 minutes remove from heat. Sprinkle sauce over pork chops and enjoy.

Russian Beef Gratin

Ingredients:

- Salt and ground black pepper, to taste
- 1 cup mozzarella cheese, shredded
- 2 cups fontina cheese, shredded
- 1 cup Russian dressing
- 2 tbsp sesame seeds, toasted
- 20 dill pickle slices
- 2 tsp onion flakes
- 2 pounds ground beef
- 2 garlic cloves, minced
- 1 iceberg lettuce head, torn

Directions:

1. Set a pan over medium heat, place in the beef, garlic, salt, onion flakes, and pepper, and cook for 5 minutes.
2. Remove and set to a baking dish, stir in half of the Russian dressing, mozzarella cheese, and spread 1 cup of the fontina cheese.
3. Lay the pickle slices on top, spread over the remaining fontina cheese and sesame seeds, place in the oven at 350ºF, and bake for 20 minutes.
4. Split the lettuce on serving plates, apply a topping of beef gratin, and the remaining Russian dressing.

Pumpkin Pie

Ingredients:

- 1/4 teaspoon ground ginger
- 1/8 teaspoon ground cloves
- 1/2 cup butter, melted
- 2 eggs
- 1/2 cup canned pumpkin puree
- 1/2 cup granulated sugar substitute
- 1/4 cup light brown sugar substitute
- 1/2 cup almond flour
- 1/4 cup coconut flour
- 1/4 teaspoon salt
- 1/4 teaspoon ground cinnamon

- 1 teaspoon vanilla extract

Directions:

1. Preheat oven to 325 degrees F (165 degrees C).
2. in a medium bowl, mix together almond flour, coconut flour, salt, cinnamon, ginger, and cloves.
3. In a large bowl, whisk together melted butter, eggs, pumpkin puree, granulated sugar substitute, light brown sugar substitute, and vanilla extract.
4. Gradually add the dry ingredients to the wet ingredients and mix until a dough forms.
5. Press the dough into a 9-inch pie plate.
6. Bake for 25-30 minutes, or until lightly golden.
7. Allow to cool before serving.

Cheesecake

Ingredients:

- 2 eggs
- 1 1/2 cups cream cheese, softened
- 1/2 cup granulated sugar substitute
- 1/4 cup light brown sugar substitute
- 1 teaspoon vanilla extract
- 1 1/2 cups almond flour
- 1/4 teaspoon salt
- 1/4 cup butter, melted
- 1/2 cup sour cream

Directions:

1. Preheat oven to 350 degrees F (175 degrees C).
2. in a medium bowl, mix together almond flour and salt.
3. In a large bowl, whisk together melted butter and eggs.
4. Add cream cheese, granulated sugar substitute, light brown sugar substitute, and vanilla extract and mix until combined.
5. Gradually add almond flour mixture to the wet ingredients and mix until combined.
6. Fold in sour cream.
7. Transfer the mixture to a 9-inch spring form pan.
8. Bake for 40-45 minutes, or until lightly golden.
9. Allow to cool before serving.

Chocolate Pudding

Ingredients:

- 1/2 cup granulated sugar substitute
- 1/4 teaspoon salt
- 4 egg yolks
- 2 tablespoons butter
- 2 cups heavy cream
- 1/2 cup cocoa powder
- 2 teaspoons vanilla extract

Directions:

1. In a medium saucepan, whisk together heavy cream, cocoa powder, sugar substitute, and salt.

2. Place saucepan over medium heat and bring to a low simmer.
3. in a separate bowl, whisk together egg yolks.
4. Gradually add a few tablespoons of the hot cream mixture to the egg yolks and whisk until combined.
5. Add the egg yolk mixture to the saucepan and cook, stirring constantly, for 5-7 minutes, or until thickened.
6. Remove from heat and stir in butter and vanilla extract.
7. Transfer the pudding to individual serving dishes.
8. Refrigerate for at least 2 hours before serving.

Baked Avocado Fries With Sriracha Mayo

Ingredients:

- 2 tsp garlic powder
- 1 tsp smoked paprika
- Salt and pepper to taste
- Two eggs, beaten (or plant-based milk for a vegan option)
- Cooking spray
- Sriracha Mayo:
- 1/2 cup of vegan mayonnaise
- 1-2 tbsp. Sriracha sauce (adjust to taste)
- 1 tsp lime juice
- 2 avocados, sliced into wedges

- 1 cup of breadcrumbs

- 1/2 cup of flour (all-purpose or almond flour for a gluten-free option)

- Salt to taste

Directions:

1. Line a baking sheet with parchment paper and set the oven to 425°F (220°C).
2. Combine the breadcrumbs, flour, garlic powder, smoked paprika, salt, and pepper in a bowl.
3. Before coating the avocado wedges with the breadcrumb mixture, dip them into the beaten eggs.
4. Next, arrange the avocado wedges coated on the ready baking sheet.
5. Apply a little coating of cooking spray to the wedges.

6. To get a golden brown and crispy texture, bake for 15 to 18 minutes.
7. Get the Sriracha Mayo ready to bake with the vegan mayonnaise, Sriracha sauce, lime juice, and salt mixed.
8. Sriracha mayo is an excellent dip for baked avocado fries.

www.ingramcontent.com/pod-product-compliance
Lightning Source LLC
LaVergne TN
LVHW010226070526
838199LV00062B/4731